Hokusai

*He saw the world
in a wave*

Written by
Susie Hodge

Illustrated by
Kim Ekdahl

"At 90, I will enter into the secret of things."

–Hokusai

Hokusai was born in 1760 and grew up to become one of the most famous Japanese artists in history. He hoped he would live to 110! He didn't quite live that long, but died in 1849, when he was 89 years old. In fact, in the Japanese way of counting he was 90, as everyone was considered to be one year old at birth.

Over his long career, Hokusai made more than 30,000 paintings, prints, and drawings. People all over the world came to know and admire the art he created.

It was common in Japan at that time for artists to use different names when they worked with a new teacher or tried a new style, but Hokusai changed his name more than most. He signed his name on prints and paintings in more than 30 different ways! Each name had a special meaning.

His name at birth was Kawamura Tokitarō, but we know him best as Katsushika Hokusai.

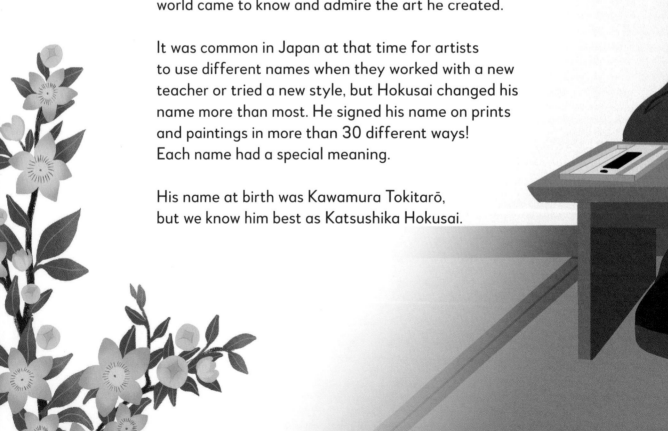

Not much is known about Hokusai's early life. His mother called him Tokitarō, which is a name usually given to a firstborn son. He grew up in Edo (now Tokyo) in Japan.

At that time, Edo was one of the largest cities in the world, with a population of over one million. The streets were always full of people—fashionable ladies, tradesmen, wealthy merchants, farmers, and children. Young women and children wore colorful kimonos, but everyone was stylish in their own way.

Hokusai was probably adopted, as was then a common practice. Hokusai's father, Nakajima Ise, was a craftsman who made mirrors with raised designs on the back. In those days, mirrors were made of bronze and the side you looked into had to be polished often. Hokusai's job was probably to help Ise polish the mirrors. He had to shine them until he could see his face in them!

Hokusai first lived in a humble wooden house on a narrow street in Edo. Over his life, it is said he moved 93 times. Some people say this was because he hated cleaning and tidying up! But Hokusai also had a restless spirit and didn't worry very much about having a comfortable house.

At the age of six, Hokusai began learning to write and draw. In Japan, drawing used many of the same skills as calligraphy, which in Japan, Korea, and China was seen as a form of art equal to painting. Both required making fluid lines using a supple-tipped brush and ink—needing lots of practice.

Hokusai loved nature. Wherever he went, he looked around and drew the shapes of what he saw—trees, mountains, hills, lakes, rivers, waterfalls, and the sea.

Copy the shapes of things you can see in nature, such as any trees, rivers, plants, or clouds.

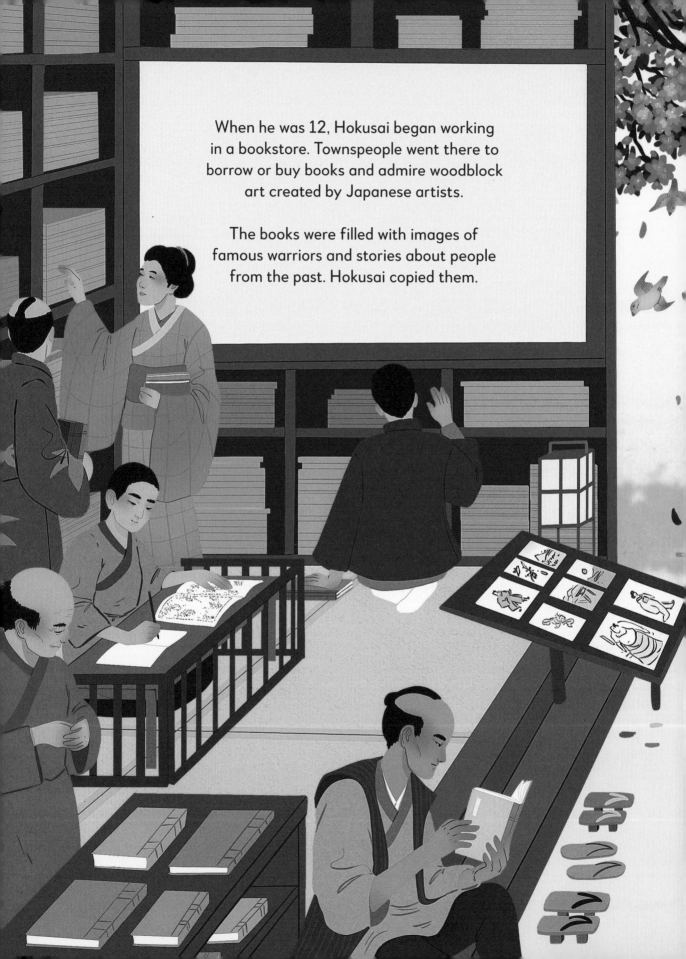

When he was 12, Hokusai began working in a bookstore. Townspeople went there to borrow or buy books and admire woodblock art created by Japanese artists.

The books were filled with images of famous warriors and stories about people from the past. Hokusai copied them.

Early in his teens, Hokusai began training in a
woodblock carver's workshop. Here he learned
to cut the cherry-wood blocks that would be
used to create the prints and book illustrations
that were so popular at this time.

Woodblock carving is a highly skilled job.
The carver pastes copies of an artist's design
onto wooden blocks, then, using sharp tools,
carves through the paper and wood, creating
the pictures and patterns that are printed.

Hokusai trained in the woodblock carver's workshop for three years. With supervision, he was allowed to cut the designs for pages of popular fiction.

Try **copying**

the work of an artist **you** *admire.*

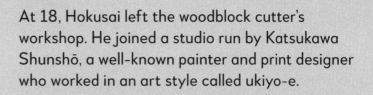

At 18, Hokusai left the woodblock cutter's workshop. He joined a studio run by Katsukawa Shunshō, a well-known painter and print designer who worked in an art style called ukiyo-e.

Ukiyo-e means "pictures of the floating world." They depict Japanese city life, showing people enjoying themselves. Ukiyo-e artists portrayed kabuki (Japanese theater) actors, sumo wrestlers, samurai (Japanese warriors) and geisha (female entertainers), folk tales, historical stories, and landscapes. Woodblock-printed ukiyo-e works were mass-produced and so were very affordable. A print cost about as much as two bowls of noodles.

Who do you see on the streets near where you live? What do they look like? What clothes do they wear? Try drawing them!

Hokusai quickly learned to create art in Shunshō's style.

With Shunshō's help, the young Hokusai was able to create wonderful images of actors, beautiful women, and wrestlers. He also made illustrations for storybooks.

All around him in Edo, Hokusai saw different people bustling about.

With elegant lines, he drew, painted, and produced prints of all he saw—including the peaceful landscapes, winding rivers, wooden bridges, and boats bobbing on the water.

Hokusai's style at this time looked like Shunshō's style of ukiyo-e. But then Hokusai also took lessons with painters Kanō Yūsen, Sumiyoshi Hiroyuki, and Tsutsumi Tōrin, who all worked in different styles.

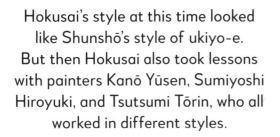

He also studied the works of ancient Chinese artists as well as Western prints, engravings, and illustrated books in which artists used perspective to make things look smaller in the distance. His own art became a blend of all these different styles.

Draw a scene of people enjoying themselves at a carnival— dancing, eating, and chatting.

During holidays and festivals, Edo was transformed into a big party with food stalls, performers, and music. Hokusai sketched all he saw because he was determined to become a better artist. At that time, most artists tried to make everything look perfect, but Hokusai wanted to make his pictures look real.

Following the Japanese custom, Katsukawa Shunshō gave his apprentice a new name: Katsukawa Shunrō. However, after a short while, Hokusai was told to stop using the name Katsukawa—perhaps because he didn't follow his teacher's style faithfully, and instead mixed different styles.

But by now, Hokusai was creating designs in his own style, which were becoming so popular with the public that people commissioned him to produce special prints for them. He made designs called surimono, which included printed calendars and greeting cards.

In 1779, aged 19, Hokusai married his first wife. Little is known about her.

Draw a **picture**
for a **calendar**,
showing one of the
seasons: spring,
summer, fall, or winter.

Japanese artists were expected to follow only one master, but Hokusai liked experimenting with different styles. "I must paint the way my heart tells me," he said. He made brush paintings and prints and illustrations for storybooks. Sometimes he wrote the stories to go with them, too.

Hokusai constantly sketched what he saw around him—people, places, and landscapes. As he did so, he developed his own individual style. His works of art showed real people and real places as he saw them.

Illustrate a story!

Draw six rectangles with pictures in each one, so people can read your story through your drawings.

In 1793, Hokusai's wife died, leaving him with their two daughters and a son.

For a short while, Hokusai changed his name to Gunbatei, then to Tawaraya Sōri, and then to Hokusai Tokimasa (sometimes pronounced Tatsumasa). In 1796, he called himself Hokusai Sōri, in honor of an artist he admired. Just a few years after that, he signed his work "Sōri aratame Hokusai," which means "Hokusai, the artist formerly known as Sōri."

By 1800, he began using the name he is now best known by: Katsushika Hokusai. Katsushika is the name of the part of Edo where he was born and Hokusai means "North Studio," after Hokushin, the Buddhist god of the North Star.

Do you know what your **name means?**
Try making a name sign for yourself and decorate it with pictures of landscapes you like to look at.

That year, he began teaching his own students.

Hokusai married his second wife in 1797.

Because he was so creative and had a great sense of humor, he became famous. And because he was famous, he was able to create all kinds of works of art and was invited to visit important people.

At a festival in Edo, using brooms and buckets of ink, he made a portrait of a monk that was so enormous it could only be seen from rooftops. Then he painted two sparrows on a tiny grain of rice.

Another time, according to legend, he was invited to the court of the Shogun for a painting contest. There, in front of an audience, he painted a river, then dipped a chicken's feet in red paint and let it run over his painting, saying that the footprints represented maple leaves floating on the Tatsuta River, near the ancient capital of Nara.

By 1804, Hokusai had four daughters as well as two sons. Hokusai's third daughter Ōi was born in 1800. Later, she became an artist, too, and rivaled her father as a skilled painter. She and her sisters all worked as Hokusai's assistants.

In the year of Ōi's birth, Hokusai published two illustrated books of local landscapes: *Famous Sights of the Eastern Capital* and *Eight Views of Edo*. For the first time, he was an independent artist, free from ties to any particular school.

During this time, Japanese people had almost no contact with anyone in the West. But secretly, Hokusai found a way to see Dutch and French engravings that had been smuggled into the country. Unlike most other Japanese artists, he was curious about art everywhere. He began designing his own landscapes inspired by Dutch art.

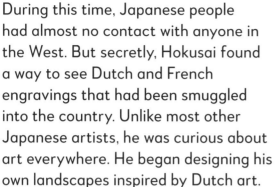

When he was 50, Hokusai was struck by lightning! Luckily, he was unharmed, but the experience certainly shocked him.

Around then, he began making drawing instruction books. His first was called *Foolish Ono's Nonsense Picture Dictionary.* These books taught readers how to draw, using shapes from basic Chinese characters, or letters.

Try creating your own **manga** or **comic-book** characters. Use just three colors, as Hokusai did.

In 1814, Hokusai began creating a series of drawing manuals. Often they included funny pictures of people and animals. He called them *Hokusai Manga* and he continued making them for the rest of his life—ending up with more than 4,000 drawings in 15 different books.

He made his manga drawings to teach others how to draw, and they continued to be published even after his death.

Printed in just three colors, Hokusai's manga drawings do not tell stories like manga or comic books today, but they do include landscapes, plants, animals, everyday life, and myths and magic.

When Hokusai turned 60, he began signing his work with the name Iitsu, which means "One Year Old Again," because he felt that he was beginning life again, just like a one-year-old child. In China and Japan, the zodiac has five cycles of 12 years each, which means from age 60 everyone starts a new life cycle.

Soon after this, his second wife died. Deeply saddened, Hokusai said prayers of remembrance and gazed at the sacred mountain of Fuji that he could just about see through the clouds.

Shaped like a perfect cone, Mount Fuji is the highest mountain in Japan. Its peak is often hidden in the clouds. To Hokusai, Mount Fuji was magical and spiritual. It inspired him, even when he was sad or tired.

He drew it at different times of day, in all seasons, and from different angles and distances. Then he made ukiyo-e prints that he called *Thirty-Six Views of Mount Fuji*. After creating these 36 pictures, he made 10 more, and, a few years later, he produced 100 more in three volumes of books!

Make a series of pictures that show the **same object**. Experiment with different sizes and compositions.

Hokusai was 70 years old when he started *Thirty-Six Views of Mount Fuji,* but he felt that he was still learning how to be a better artist.

Hokusai's most famous print is *Under the Wave off Kanagawa*, better known as *The Great Wave.* It is an image of a gigantic wave curling in the air, about to crash onto three small fishing boats. Tiny men row the boats, showing the great size of the wave. Mount Fuji can just be seen in the background under the curl of the wave. Storm clouds hang in the sky around Mount Fuji's snowy, sacred peak.

Hokusai wanted to show people the beauty that he saw in nature, and particularly the sacred mountain.

With his new ideas and images, Hokusai changed Japanese art.

He had loved drawing nature all his life, and now people admired his pictures of plants, trees, people, animals, water, and mountains.

Other artists followed him, no longer creating so many pictures of actors, wrestlers, or beautiful women. Instead, they copied Hokusai's style of art!

What do you like most about Hokusai's art?

When he was 74, Hokusai changed his name to Gakyō Rōjin Manji, meaning "Old Man Mad about Painting."

Hokusai's daughter Ōi moved in with him, so she could help him and work on her own art, but when he was 79, a fire in his studio destroyed much of his work. Then his grandson lost a lot of Hokusai's money. Hokusai and Ōi had to leave their home and move into a temple.

But Hokusai did not let any of this stop him from making art. He was determined to keep drawing, painting, and printmaking as long as he lived.

Just before he died close to the age of 90, Hokusai said: "If heaven would give me just five more years, I might become a true painter."

No matter how successful he became, or how many people admired his art, Hokusai always thought that he could improve. For the whole of his life, he worked hard, always closely studying the subjects he wanted to draw.

Hokusai inspired Japanese artists to experiment more, while international artists collected his prints and learned from his ideas, developing new art styles. In France, the fashion for Japanese art became known as Japonisme. Hokusai's *Manga* was even used as a drawing manual by later artists known as Impressionists and Post-Impressionists.

His influence continues to this day.

Try to draw in the Japanese way! Use a black ballpoint pen and hold it upright with your paper flat on a table. Draw lines to make a picture of a tree in front and a mountain in the distance.

Timeline of key artworks

A great experimenter, Hokusai created art for more than 70 years, making designs for book illustrations and woodblock prints, sketches, and paintings.

Here are a few of his key works from that time, all in the collection of The Metropolitan Museum of Art.

c. 1815

Transmitting the Spirit, Revealing the Form of Things, Volume 1 of Hokusai's sketchbooks; Woodblock printed book; ink and color on paper

1814

Two Women and a Boy Visiting a Shrine in Meguro; Woodblock print (surimono); ink and color on paper

c. 1793

The Sumo Wrestlers; Woodblock print; ink and color on paper

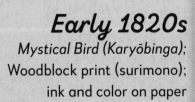

Early 1820s

Mystical Bird (Karyōbinga); Woodblock print (surimono); ink and color on paper

> ## "When I am 80, you will see real progress."
> –Hokusai

1827–1833
The Amida Falls in the Far Reaches of the Kisokaidō Road (Kisoji no oku Amida-ga-taki), from the series A Tour of Waterfalls in Various Provinces (Shokoku taki meguri); Woodblock print; ink and color on paper

Early 1830s
Rooster, Hen and Chicken with Spiderwort; Woodblock print; ink and color on paper

1831
Under the Wave off Kanagawa; Woodblock print; ink and color on paper

Timeline continued:

1831

Ejiri in Suruga Province (Sunshū Ejiri), from the series *Thirty-Six Views of Mount Fuji (Fugaku sanjūrokkei);* Woodblock print; ink and color on paper

1832

Nihonbashi in Edo (Edo Nihonbashi), from the series *Thirty-Six Views of Mount Fuji (Fugaku sanjūrokkei);* Woodblock print; ink and color on paper

1833

Fuji from Gotenyama on the Tōkaidō at Shinagawa (Tōkaidō Shinagawa Gotenyama no Fuji), from the series *Thirty-Six Views of Mount Fuji (Fugaku sanjūrokkei);* Woodblock print; ink and color on paper

c. 1830–1833

The Waterwheel at Onden (Onden no suisha), from the series *Thirty-Six Views of Mount Fuji (Fugaku sanjūrokkei)*; Woodblock print; ink and color on paper

1833–1834

Cranes on Branch of Snow-Covered Pine; Woodblock print; ink and color on paper

"Since my sixth year, I have had a burning desire to draw all things."

–Hokusai, 1834

Late 1830s

Poem by Ise, from the series *One Hundred Poems Explained by the Nurse*; Woodblock print; ink and color on paper

Make a great wave

Under the Wave off Kanagawa (Kanagawa-oki Nami Ura), usually just called *The Great Wave*, is the most well-known work of Japanese art in the world. Many people have copied or been inspired by it. It even has its own emoji! Now you can copy it, too, in your own unique way.

Look at the picture carefully. What do you see? The big wave and the tiny mountain in the background are perfectly balanced. Here, Hokusai combined ideas of Japanese art with Western ideas about perspective—making things look far away or close up. The foam of the wave looks like claws, grasping for the fishermen in their boats. The biggest wave forms a round frame for Mount Fuji in the distance.

Under the Wave off Kanagawa, 1831, woodcut

Yin and yang is a belief that began in ancient China and spread to Japan, meaning opposites that are seen everywhere, for instance, dark and light, night and day, large and small. In *The Great Wave*, the large (wet) wave is yin and the empty (dry) air below is yang.

Now you try: Create your own collage of *The Great Wave!*

Create your own version ...

Use recycled materials—for example, newspaper, wrapping paper, cotton balls, tissue paper, cutouts from magazines. Tear and cut your shapes, then layer them. What will you stick down first?

Things that are farthest away, such as Mount Fuji itself, might need to be stuck first. The sea needs to be layered, and the little boats should be stuck on last.

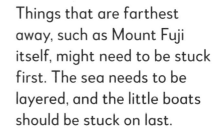

Produce your own prints

Hokusai made many woodcut prints, experimenting with line, color, and composition. You can make your own simple prints with fruit and vegetables, such as potatoes, apples, or carrots. When you make a print, your pattern or picture will end up back to front, so think about this when you design it. Hokusai is famous for painting nature, so make your print of something natural—you could choose flowers, trees, plants, animals, and more ...

Fuji from Gotenyama on the Tōkaidō at Shinagawa (Tōkaidō Shinagawa Gotenyama no Fuji), from the series Thirty-Six Views of Mount Fuji (Fugaku sanjūrokkei), 1833, Woodblock print; ink and color on paper

Try this yourself!

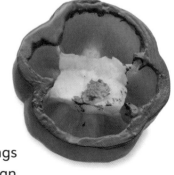

Have a go yourself! Many things will work to make a print: You can carefully cut up a sponge, a potato, or other vegetables, or recycle a material such as thick cardboard.

> *"At 73, I began to understand the true construction of animals, plants, trees, birds, fishes, and insects."*
>
> –Hokusai

If you are cutting into something hard such as a potato, an adult will need to help. Cut the object in half and draw on the flat surface with an old ballpoint pen, then carve out your shape.

Spread paint on the surface of your finished design and get printing.

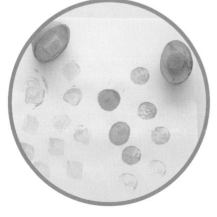

Step back and admire your finished artwork!

Glossary

apprentice (*noun*)
Someone who works for somebody else to learn that person's skill or trade. Apprentices are usually young and learning from older, more experienced people.

calligraphy (*noun*)
Beautiful handwriting created with a supple-tipped brush in East Asia, but with a quill or pen elsewhere in the world.

composition (*noun*)
How an artist decides to position things in or on an artwork.

engraving (*noun*)
A type of print created using a cutting tool and metal plates.

Impressionists (*noun*)
A group of late 19th-century artists who painted scenes of everyday life with lively brushwork and vivid color and paid special attention to the changing effects of light.

Japonisme (*noun*)
A French term made up in the late 19th century to describe the huge fashion for Japanese art and design in Europe and America.

manga *(noun)*

A type of contemporary Japanese graphic novel or comic book. Hokusai used the word *manga* to mean "random sketches" of everything imaginable in the world around him. Both *Hokusai Manga* and today's manga rely on cartoonlike images drawn in a lively manner.

ukiyo-e *(noun)*

A Japanese art form from the 17th–19th centuries meaning "pictures of the floating world." The "e" refers to pictures and "ukiyo" means pleasures—including theaters, actors, wrestlers, dancers, and beautiful women.

perspective *(noun)*

The technique used to depict something three-dimensional, such as a building or a person, on a flat surface.

Post-Impressionists *(noun)*

Artists who followed the Impressionists, using brighter colors and distortions for more expressive effects.

Shogun *(noun)*

A Japanese military commander.

woodblock *(noun)*

A Japanese printmaking technique. The artist carves the surface of a wooden block, then spreads ink over it with a roller. A sheet of paper is placed on top and rubbed with a tool. The paper is then peeled off. For prints with several colors, the artist makes a block for each color.

Susie Hodge

Susie Hodge, MA, FRSA, is an art historian, artist, and award-winning author with more than 150 books published, mainly on art and design history, practical art, and history. She also writes magazine articles and web resources for museums and galleries, and provides workshops and lectures for schools, universities, museums, galleries, businesses, festivals, and societies around the world. She has taught in schools and colleges and is a regular contributor to radio and TV documentaries and news programs. She began her career as a copywriter in advertising.

Kim Ekdahl

Kim is a freelance illustrator based in Sweden. She has roots in game development, which made her realize her love for creating unique characters and telling enchanting stories with her art. When she's not illustrating, she enjoys playing games, reading fantasy or sci-fi novels, and taking care of her plants, which are all things that inspire her art greatly. Working on this book has rekindled her love of Japanese art.

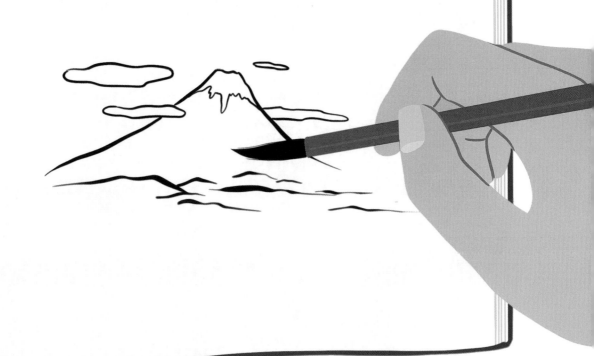

Senior Editor Emma Grange
Senior Designer Anna Formanek
Project Editor Rosie Peet
Designer Clare Baggaley
Picture Researchers Martin Copeland
and Vagisha Pushp
Production Editor Siu Yin Chan
Senior Production Controller Louise Minihane
Senior Acquisitions Editor Katy Flint
Managing Editor Paula Regan
Managing Art Editors Jo Connor and Vicky Short
Publishing Director Mark Searle

First American Edition, 2021
Published in the United States by DK Publishing
1450 Broadway, Suite 801, New York, NY 10018

Page design copyright © 2021 Dorling Kindersley Limited
DK, a Division of Penguin Random House LLC
21 22 23 24 25 10 9 8 7 6 5 4 3 2
003–322792–Nov/2021

 **The Metropolitan
Museum of Art**
New York

© The Metropolitan Museum of Art

A catalog record for this book
is available from the Library of Congress.
ISBN 978-0-7440-3978-8

DK books are available at special discounts when purchased in bulk for sales
promotions, premiums, fund-raising, or educational use. For details, contact:
DK Publishing Special Markets,
1450 Broadway, Suite 801, New York, NY 10018
SpecialSales@dk.com

Printed and bound in China

Acknowledgments
DK would like to thank John Carpenter, Mike Hearn, Lisa
Silverman Meyers, Laura Barth, Leanne Graeff, Emily Blumenthal,
and Morgan Pearce at The Met; Hilary Becker; Clare Baggaley;
Jennette ElNaggar at DK; and Susie Hodge and Kim Ekdahl.

For the curious

www.dk.com
www.metmuseum.org

Picture credits

The publisher would like to thank The Metropolitan Museum of Art for their kind permission to reproduce and illustrate works of art from their collection and the following for additional permission to reproduce their photographs:

(Key: a-above; b-below/bottom; c-center; f-far; l-left; r-right; t-top)

Dreamstime.com: Martijn Mulder / Martijnmulder 45br, Teen00000 45cla, 45cl
Shutterstock.com: Quirky Mundo 40-41, 42-43 (Background)
The Metropolitan Museum of Art: *The Sumo Wrestlers Takaneyama Yoichiemon and Sendagawa Kichigorō*, c. 1793, Katsushika Hokusai. The Francis Lathrop Collection, Purchase, Frederick C. Hewitt Fund, 1911. JP741 40tl; *Two Women and a Boy Visiting a Shrine in Meguro*, 1814, Katsushika Hokusai. H. O. Havemeyer Collection, Bequest of Mrs. H. O. Havemeyer, 1929. JP2019 40tc; *Transmitting the Spirit, Revealing the Form of Things, Volume 1 to 15 of Hokusai Sketchbooks*, Volume 1, c. 1815, Katsushika Hokusai. The Howard Mansfield Collection, Gift of Howard Mansfield, 1936. JIB111a–k 40tr; *Mystical Bird (Karyōbinga)*, early 1820s, Katsushika Hokusai. H. O. Havemeyer Collection, Bequest of Mrs. H. O. Havemeyer, 1929. JP1868 40br; *The Amida Falls in the Far Reaches of the Kisokaidō Road (Kisoji no oku Amida-ga-taki)*, from the series *A Tour of Waterfalls in Various Provinces (Shokoku taki meguri)* 1827–1833, Katsushika Hokusai. The Francis Lathrop Collection, Purchase, Frederick C. Hewitt Fund, 1911. JP745 41tr; *Rooster, Hen and Chicken with Spiderwort*, early 1830s, Katsushika Hokusai. Museum Accession. JP1085 41tl; *Under the Wave off Kanagawa (Kanagawa oki nami ura)*, also known as *The Great Wave*, from the series *Thirty-Six Views of Mount Fuji (Fugaku sanjūrokkei)*, 1831, Katsushika Hokusai. H. O. Havemeyer Collection, Bequest of Mrs. H. O. Havemeyer, 1929. JP1047 41bl, 44c; *Ejiri in Suruga Province (Sunshū Ejiri)*, from the series *Thirty-Six Views of Mount Fuji (Fugaku sanjūrokkei)*, 1831, Katsushika Hokusai. The Howard Mansfield Collection, Purchase, Rogers Fund, 1936. JP2553 42tr; *Nihonbashi in Edo (Edo Nihonbashi)*, from the series *Thirty-Six Views of Mount Fuji (Fugaku sanjūrokkei)*, c. 1832, Katsushika Hokusai. Henry L. Phillips Collection, Bequest of Henry L. Phillips, 1939. JP2993 42cl; *Fuji from Gotenyama on the Tōkaidō at Shinagawa (Tōkaidō Shinagawa Gotenyama no Fuji)*, from the series *Thirty-Six Views of Mount Fuji (Fugaku sanjūrokkei)*, 1833, Katsushika Hokusai. Rogers Fund, 1922. JP1284 42br, 46tl; *The Waterwheel at Onden (Onden no suisha)*, from the series *Thirty-Six Views of Mount Fuji (Fugaku sanjūrokkei)*, c. 1830–1833, Katsushika Hokusai. Henry L. Phillips Collection, Bequest of Henry L. Phillips, 1939. JP2967 42tl; *Cranes on Branch of Snow-Covered Pine*, 1833–1834, Katsushika Hokusai. The Francis Lathrop Collection, Purchase, Frederick C. Hewitt Fund, 1911. JP660 42cr; *Poem by Ise*, from the series *One Hundred Poems Explained by the Nurse (Hyakunin isshu uba ga etoki)*, late 1830s, Katsushika Hokusai. Rogers Fund, 1922. JP1340 42bl.